ALL ABOUT
RUBBER DUCKS
ORIGINS, FUN, COLLECTIONS

Diane Schildgen
John Kilbride

ISBN 9798879828962

Second Edition

For Uncle Dan, who loves his rubber ducks.

This Book Belongs To

----

*Dive into the enchanting world of rubber ducks with **All About Rubber Ducks.** Uncover the fascinating history, cultural impact, and unexpected adventures of these beloved bath-time companions.*

From their humble origins to becoming pop culture icons, follow the quack-tastic journey of rubber ducks across continents. Explore the thrill of rubber duck races, where each quack echoes for a cause.

Immerse yourself in the whimsical tales of passionate collectors and the unique personalities of these friends.

Chapter One
A Splash Through History

As we embark on this delightful rubber duck adventure, we are set to unravel the captivating tale of these cheerful bath-time companions. From their humble origins to achieving the status of cultural icons, the evolution of rubber ducks is a quacky journey that spans centuries, captivating hearts around the globe.

Evolution: From Rigid to Resilient

Our journey commences in the early 19th century, a time when rubber ducks were far from the squeezable, floatable companions we know today. During this era, bath-time toys took on a different form – solid, rigid figures made from various materials, lacking the iconic duck shape we associate with them today. The transformative moment arrived in the 1940s with the introduction of soft rubber, marking a turning point in the history of rubber ducks.

Visualize the innovation that birthed the modern rubber duck – resilient, buoyant, and ready to face the challenges of bath time with a cheerful bounce. This evolution marked a new era for rubber ducks, endearing them to millions as squishy, lovable

6

playmates. The transition from rigid to resilient mirrored the whimsy and adaptability that define the essence of rubber ducks.

Design Changes: Runway Stars of the Tub

Rubber ducks have graced the metaphorical runway more times than Hollywood stars on a red carpet. The design studio of rubber ducks is a haven of creativity, and over the years, these bath-time companions have embraced a kaleidoscope of changes. Transitioning from the classic yellow hue, they have evolved into dazzling arrays of colors and patterns, turning bath time into a miniature fashion show.

Picture a rubber duck runway where each duck struts its stuff – some sporting funky sunglasses, others donning cool hats. Design changes weren't merely cosmetic; they infused each duck with its distinctive personality, transforming them into miniature works of art. The bathtub became a stage, and rubber ducks, the stars, captured the spotlight with their ever-changing styles.

Role in Popular Culture: Quacks on the Big Stage

The ascent of rubber ducks from mere toys to cultural symbols is a testament to their enduring charm. Who could forget Ernie's iconic "Rubber

Duckie" song on Sesame Street, a tune that echoed through households and became a timeless anthem for bath time? The thrilling bathtub races further cemented the status of rubber ducks as more than just bath-time companions.

These little yellow wonders transcended their bath-time origins to become cultural icons, making appearances in movies, commercials, and even gracing the halls of art museums as sculptures and paintings. The rubber duck's ability to transcend the boundaries of the bathroom turned it into a pop culture sensation.

They are not just ducks; they are the rockstars of the bathroom, and their fame knows no bounds.

A notable event that thrust rubber ducks into the global spotlight was the "Giant Yellow Rubber Duck Project" by Dutch artist Florentijn Hofman. This ambitious project featured a massive inflatable rubber duck showcased in various global locations, drawing large crowds and extensive media coverage. The giant rubber duck, with its whimsical presence, created a sense of wonder and joy, captivating people of all ages.

As we sail through the rich history of rubber ducks, be prepared for more surprises than bubbles in a bubble bath. The journey of these whimsical bath-time companions continues to unfold, weaving a narrative that spans generations and captures the hearts of enthusiasts worldwide. Stay tuned for the next chapter, where the rubber duck adventure takes an unexpected turn into uncharted waters, promising more quack-tastic tales and discoveries.

Chapter Two

The Duck Factory Chronicles - Unveiling the Craftsmanship

As we dive deeper into the enchanting world of rubber ducks, our journey takes a fascinating turn toward the very heart of their creation – the Duck Factory. Picture a place where creativity dances with craftsmanship, and the process of bringing these adorable bath-time companions to life unfolds like a magical tale.

The Rubber Duck Manufacturing Process: A Symphony of Transformation

Why focus on rubber ducks, you might wonder? Well, my friend, these are not your ordinary bath toys; they are like tiny superheroes in the realm of fun. Join me on a cool adventure as we explore why people from every corner of the globe go bananas for rubber ducks. These little quackers aren't just meant for splashing around in the tub; they have a tale to tell!

In the early 19th century, rubber ducks were a far cry from the soft, squeezable, and duck-shaped toys we know today. They existed as solid, rigid creations crafted from various materials. However, the game-changing moment arrived in the 1940s with the invention of soft rubber, ushering in a new era for these bath-time companions. Suddenly, rubber ducks became not only squeezable and floatable but also the lovable icons we cherish today.

The transformation of these once rigid toys into soft, huggable companions mirrors the whimsy and adaptability that define the rubber duck's essence.

Design Changes: A Fashion Show for Ducks

The world of rubber ducks is dynamic, akin to a glamorous movie star's ever-changing wardrobe. The design studio of rubber ducks is a hub where creativity flows freely, resulting in a myriad of makeovers that could make even the fanciest fashionistas jealous. From the classic yellow hue to an array of colors and patterns, these ducks have strutted their stuff in countless styles, evolving with the times.

Imagine a rubber duck fashion show where each duck proudly displays its unique look – some adorned with funky sunglasses, others sporting cool hats. Design changes weren't merely cosmetic; they bestowed upon each duck its own awesome personality, transforming bath time into a playground of individuality and expression.

The Role in Popular Culture: Ducks as Icons

Who could forget Ernie's timeless "Rubber Duckie" song on Sesame Street or the captivating bathtub races that captured the imaginations of people worldwide? These little yellow wonders transcended their status as mere toys; they evolved into cultural symbols, making appearances in movies, commercials, and even finding their way into art sculptures and paintings displayed in prestigious museums.

The rubber duck's ability to transcend the boundaries of the bathroom turned it into a pop culture icon, spreading joy and nostalgia far beyond the confines of the tub.

One notable event that thrust rubber ducks into the spotlight is the "Giant Yellow Rubber Duck Project" by Dutch artist Florentijn Hofman. This ambitious project involves showcasing a massive inflatable rubber duck in various locations worldwide, attracting large crowds and extensive media coverage. The giant rubber duck, with its whimsical presence, creates a sense of wonder and joy, captivating people of all ages and reminding us of the infectious happiness these simple bath-time companions bring.

The Duck Factory Chronicles: Crafting Joyful Quackers

Now, let's take a step into the enchanting world of the Duck Factory, where the magic happens. This is the birthplace of rubber ducks, where skilled artisans and cutting-edge technology come together to craft these delightful quackers. The manufacturing process is a symphony of creativity, precision, and a dash of quirkiness.

It all begins with the selection of high-quality, safe materials. Soft rubber, the hero of the show, ensures that each duck is not just a toy but a companion that can withstand the waters of countless bath times. The rubber sheets are carefully cut into duck shapes, laying the foundation for the iconic silhouette.

But it's not just about the shape; it's about the personality. The design phase brings forth a burst of creativity, as artists sketch and mold each duck into a unique character. From playful expressions to whimsical accessories, every detail is considered to ensure that each rubber duck has its own charm.

The manufacturing process involves a combination of traditional craftsmanship and modern techniques. Injection molding machines bring the duck shapes to life, injecting them with the vibrant colors that make them stand out in the tub. The ducks then take a joyful journey through a series of quality checks, ensuring that they meet the highest standards of safety and durability.

But the Duck Factory isn't just about mass production; it's about infusing joy into every quacker. Skilled artisans add final touches by hand, ensuring that each duck is a work of art. From hand-painting intricate details to attaching accessories, these artisans bring the ducks to life with a personal touch.

As the ducks waddle off the production line, they are ready to embark on their mission – spreading smiles and turning ordinary bath times into quack-tastic adventures. The Duck Factory, with its blend of craftsmanship and whimsy, stands as a testament to the dedication of those who bring these little companions to life.

Our journey through the rubber duck's world has only just begun. Stay tuned for the next chapter, where we'll explore the diverse and surprising world of rubber duck collectors. Get ready to quack on as our adventure unfolds, revealing more tales of joy, creativity, and the irresistible charm of rubber ducks.

Chapter Three

Racing with the Quacks - A Quack-tastic Odyssey

As we plunge into the vibrant realm of rubber duck races, envision a world where waters shimmer with anticipation, and the jubilant echoes of quacks resonate like cheers from an exuberant crowd. Join us on an exhilarating journey as we unfurl the quack-tastic tales of these races – from their modest beginnings to achieving global renown, where rubber ducks gracefully navigate downstream, not just for glory but for a noble cause.

Origins and Driving Forces: Quack-tastic Beginnings

The narrative of rubber duck races unfurls like a whimsical storybook, painting picturesque scenes of small towns nestled along meandering rivers. In these charming locales, a playful idea takes flight – the notion to let rubber ducks embark on downstream races. The impetus behind these races is as simple as it is profound: pure, unadulterated fun. It's a quirky endeavor aimed at bringing communities together and injecting an extra dose of excitement into mundane, everyday life.

What commences as a lighthearted pastime soon transforms into a force for good. Charitable causes weave their way into the fabric of rubber duck races, elevating these events from mere spectacles to avenues for community engagement and philanthropy.

The joy of racing rubber ducks becomes a conduit for supporting charities, turning seemingly simple races into powerful tools for making a positive splash in the world. The quacks, once mere echoes in the river, now resonate with a deeper purpose, guiding the way towards meaningful impact and communal unity.

Rise in Popularity: Quacking Around the Globe

The quacky phenomenon that begins as a small-town spectacle quickly gains momentum, and rubber duck races spread their wings, quacking their way into cities and towns across the globe. The infectious spirit of these races transcends borders, capturing hearts worldwide and transforming rubber duck races into a universal symbol of joy and charitable giving.

The surge in popularity transcends the mere act of racing rubber ducks; it transforms into a movement. People from diverse corners of the world yearn to be part of the quacky fun, not just for the thrill of the race, but also to support charities and community projects. The quacks of rubber ducks morph into a unifying sound, echoing a collective desire to contribute to a better world while reveling in a quacking good time.

Famous Races: Quack-tastic Spectacles

Now, let's immerse ourselves in the grandeur of the big leagues of rubber duck races – the illustrious ones that draw crowds, create quack-fueled frenzies, and turn serene waterways into quack-tastic spectacles.

Visualize the Great Quack-Off Spectacle, an annual extravaganza that metamorphoses a tranquil river into a riot of colors. Thousands of rubber ducks, adorned in vibrant hues, elegantly race downstream. Spectators cheer for their adopted ducks, and the excitement builds with every quack as the rubber ducks bob along, neck and neck in a spirited race to the finish. This iconic race doesn't just entertain; it serves as a testament to the potent combination of joy and community celebration.

The Grand Quackington Canal Race, hosted in the heart of a bustling city, turns a typically calm canal into a lively racecourse. The urban landscape provides a distinctive backdrop, creating a quack-tastic spectacle that magnetically draws both locals and visitors alike. It's not merely a race; it's a fusion of city life, waterways, and the infectious enthusiasm of rubber duck aficionados.

Now, let your imagination soar to the Charity Quack-a-thon, where rubber ducks don't merely race for glory but also for a cause. This prestigious race collaborates with multiple charities, transforming the event into a robust fundraiser for a myriad of causes, from education to environmental conservation. The quacks become a rallying cry for positive change, rendering every race more than just a competition – it's a collective effort to make a meaningful impact.

In the International Quack Derby, rubber duck enthusiasts from every corner of the globe converge to witness this spectacular event. Participants adopt ducks representing different countries, transforming the race into a powerful symbol of unity and international camaraderie. The event transcends geographical boundaries, bringing together individuals from diverse backgrounds under the universal banner of rubber duck enthusiasm.

There you have it – the enthralling history, the meteoric rise in popularity, and the enchantment of famous rubber duck races. These events are not mere competitions; they are grand celebrations of community, compassion, and the quack-tastic spirit that gracefully flows through the waters, leaving smiles in its wake. Prepare to quack on as our rubber duck adventure races ahead, promising to unveil more tales of joy, charity, and the quacking wonders that define these extraordinary events!

The Quack-tastic Impact on Communities: Racing for a Cause

As rubber duck races transcended their humble beginnings, their impact on communities became increasingly profound. Beyond the joyous quacks and the thrill of the race, these events evolved into powerful tools for social change and philanthropy. The concept of racing rubber ducks downstream became a creative and entertaining means to raise funds for charitable causes, turning each event into a community-wide celebration with a purpose.

Charitable organizations and community groups saw an opportunity to harness the enthusiasm generated by rubber duck races for the greater good. The quack-tastic races became fundraisers, drawing participants and spectators alike who were eager to contribute to various charitable endeavors. Whether it was supporting local schools, healthcare initiatives, or environmental conservation projects, rubber duck races provided a unique platform to channel community energy towards positive and impactful causes.

The symbiotic relationship between rubber duck races and charitable efforts became a hallmark of these events. Local businesses often sponsored rubber ducks, contributing to the fundraising efforts and further integrating the community into the race festivities. The sense of collective participation, coupled with the festive atmosphere surrounding the races, fostered a spirit of unity and shared responsibility.

As rubber duck races continued to quack their way into the hearts of communities globally, their charitable impact expanded exponentially. The funds raised through these races began to make tangible differences in the lives of those in need. Educational programs flourished, environmental conservation initiatives gained momentum, and essential community services received vital support – all fueled by the quacks of rubber ducks racing for a cause.

The Globalization of Quackery: Beyond Borders

What started as a quaint local tradition in small towns soon transformed into a global phenomenon. Rubber duck races, once confined to the tranquil waters of neighborhood rivers, began to transcend geographical boundaries. The infectious spirit of quackery spread far and wide, captivating diverse cultures and communities.

International Rubber Duck Derbies emerged, drawing participants and spectators from different continents. The races became a symbol of cross-cultural unity, bringing people together under the banner of rubber duck enthusiasm. Each rubber duck, adorned with colors and symbols representing various nations, symbolized a shared commitment to joy, charity, and the collective pursuit of making a positive impact in the world.

Global events, such as the International Quack Derby, turned into celebrations of diversity and camaraderie. Participants proudly adopted rubber ducks that represented their countries, infusing the races with a rich tapestry of cultural elements. The shared experience of watching rubber ducks gracefully glide downstream became a universal language, transcending linguistic and cultural barriers.

The globalization of quackery also led to the exchange of ideas and innovations among communities worldwide. Organizers from different regions shared insights on hosting successful rubber duck races, from fundraising strategies to event logistics. This collaborative spirit enhanced the quality and impact of these events, further solidifying rubber duck races as a global force for good.

Quacking into the Future: The Enduring Legacy

As we reflect on the quack-tastic odyssey of rubber duck races, it becomes evident that these events have woven themselves into the fabric of communities across the globe. What started as a playful pastime in small-town rivers has evolved into a powerful force for positive change, leaving an enduring legacy of joy, unity, and philanthropy.

The enduring appeal of rubber duck races lies not only in the thrill of the race but in their ability to bring people together for a shared cause. Communities, regardless of size or location, have embraced the quack-tastic spirit, turning rubber duck races into annual traditions that transcend generations. Families gather along riverbanks, friends cheer for their adopted ducks, and local businesses proudly support these events, knowing they contribute to the well-being of their communities.

Looking ahead, the future of rubber duck races appears to be as bright as the vibrant hues that adorn the racing ducks. With continued innovation, creative fundraising efforts, and a commitment to charitable causes, these quack-tastic events are poised to make an even greater impact. As new generations join the tradition, the quacks of rubber ducks will continue to echo through rivers, creating ripples of joy and positive change that extend far beyond the water's edge.

So, let us quack on, dear readers, into the future where rubber duck races remain a testament to the remarkable ability of communities to come together, have a quacking good time, and make a meaningful splash in the world. As our rubber duck adventure continues, join us in exploring more tales of joy, charity, and the quacking wonders that define these extraordinary events!

Chapter 4

Quack Treasures - The World of Rubber Duck Collectors

In the vast and whimsical universe of rubber ducks, a unique and passionate community thrives – the collectors. These enthusiasts embark on a delightful journey, turning bath-time companions into cherished treasures, each duck holding a personal story. Whether it's a vintage duck passed down from a grandparent or a limited-edition find from a memorable trip, the world of rubber duck collectors is a tapestry woven with joy, connection, and a splash of celebrity ducks.

Reason for Starting a Collection

Why do people decide to collect rubber ducks? It's not merely about accumulating bath-time buddies; it's a journey ignited by joy and a desire to connect with the playful side of life. For many collectors, the odyssey commences with a single duck, serving as a gateway to capture and preserve the simple joys of childhood. Picture a collector reminiscing about the first duck they ever owned or the one gifted by a dear friend. For these collectors, it's not just about the ducks themselves; it's about the memories they evoke and the connections they symbolize.

The decision to start a rubber duck collection often stems from a deep appreciation for the whimsical and nostalgic aspects of these bath-time companions. Collectors find a sense of joy and comfort in surrounding themselves with these quack-tastic treasures, transforming their spaces into havens of playfulness and memories. The journey of collecting is a celebration of the carefree moments of youth, an endeavor to capture and encapsulate the essence of innocent delight found in the simplest of toys – the rubber duck.

How to Start Collecting

Curious about starting your own rubber duck collection? Fear not; it's simpler than you might think. Begin with just one duck. Let your collection burgeon by exploring different colors, sizes, and themes. Dive into local stores, online marketplaces, and specialty shops catering to rubber duck enthusiasts. The key is to follow your quacky instincts and let your collection grow one duck at a time, each addition telling a unique tale.

Starting a rubber duck collection is an organic and personal experience. There are no strict rules or guidelines; collectors are free to let their preferences guide them. Some may be drawn to specific themes, such as ducks dressed as historical figures or representing different professions, creating a curated collection that tells a story. Others may focus on acquiring rare or vintage ducks, adding a layer of uniqueness to their collection.

The joy of collecting lies in the journey, the thrill of discovering a new duck that sparks delight. Rubber duck enthusiasts find treasures in unexpected places – a quaint local store, a flea market, or an online auction. Each addition to the collection brings a sense of accomplishment and adds a quack-tastic touch to the collector's story.

Celebrity Ducks

Ever dreamed of having a rubber duck that shares the fame of your favorite celebrity? Enter the realm of celebrity ducks, adorned with the likeness of famous people, becoming prized possessions for collectors.

From musicians to beloved actors, these ducks bring a touch of stardom to the bathtub. Celebrity ducks add a playful twist to collections, turning them into miniature showcases of pop culture and allowing collectors to bask in the whimsy of their favorite stars during bath time.

The allure of celebrity ducks goes beyond their famous faces; they become conversation starters and cherished pieces of memorabilia. Imagine regaling guests with tales of your celebrity rubber duck collection, each duck representing a beloved icon. These ducks bridge the gap between popular culture and the intimate world of bath-time relaxation, adding a dash of glamour to the often mundane act of bathing.

Conventions

Rubber duck collectors converge at conventions to celebrate their quacky passion. These gatherings transcend the mere act of buying and selling; they are about sharing stories, discovering rare finds, and connecting with fellow enthusiasts. Picture a convention hall abuzz with energy – collectors from all walks of life, their faces lighting up at the sight of rare ducks and unique finds. Participants engage in lively conversations, swapping stories about prized acquisitions and discovering new treasures. It's a universal language of rubber ducks that unites collectors in their shared passion.

Rubber duck conventions serve as epicenters of quackery, providing collectors with a unique opportunity to immerse themselves in a world where their passion takes center stage. These events showcase the diversity of rubber duck collections, from the charmingly simple to the exquisitely intricate. Enthusiasts peruse vendor booths, eager to uncover rare ducks and exchange insights with fellow collectors.

Past Locations

The International Rubber Duck Convention has become a migratory pattern of quack-filled gatherings, traversing continents and adding unique flavors to each location. Each convention becomes a global celebration of rubber duck friendships, creating lasting memories and strengthening the bonds within the collector community.

The choice of convention locations adds a dynamic element to the experience. Different cities and countries bring their unique charm to the gathering, offering collectors the chance to explore diverse cultures while sharing their love for rubber ducks. Whether it's a convention by the serene seaside or one amid the hustle and bustle of a vibrant metropolis, each location leaves an indelible mark on the quack-tastic tapestry of the rubber duck collecting community.

Participants

Envision a diverse array of collectors filling a convention hall – from the passionate individual who began their collection with a single duck to the seasoned enthusiast with shelves adorned in quackery. Rubber duck conventions provide a space for all to come together, celebrating the joy of collecting and sharing the thrill of discovering a new duck.

Enthusiasts scour local stores, flea markets, and online marketplaces, always on the lookout for the next addition to their quackery. Some collectors focus on specific themes, creating curated collections that tell a unique and quack-tastic story.

The participant spectrum at rubber duck conventions reflects the inclusive nature of this hobby. Whether you're a novice collector eagerly exploring your first convention or a seasoned aficionado sharing insights with fellow enthusiasts, the camaraderie is palpable. Conversations flow effortlessly as collectors swap stories, offer advice, and marvel at the diverse array of rubber ducks on display.

So, whether you're just starting your collection or already have a bathtub overflowing with ducks, remember – in the world of rubber ducks, every collection tells a quack-tastic story, and each duck holds a treasure trove of memories waiting to be discovered.

Events

Finding rubber duck events is a delightful adventure for enthusiasts seeking to immerse themselves in the quacky world of collectors. While specific events may vary from year to year, here are some general tips and places to explore when searching for rubber duck conventions:

Online Platforms: Keep an eye on popular online event platforms. Search using keywords like "rubber duck convention" or "duck collector meetup" to narrow down relevant events.

Rubber Duck Communities and Forums: Engage with online communities and forums dedicated to rubber duck enthusiasts. Websites like Rubber Duck Talk or collector forums may have announcements or discussions about upcoming conventions. Members of these communities often share information about events they plan to attend or have heard about.

Social Media Groups: Join social media groups or pages related to rubber duck collecting. Follow official pages of organizations or groups that host or sponsor rubber duck-related events.

Toy and Collectible Shows: Explore general toy and collectible conventions or shows. While not exclusively focused on rubber ducks, these events may feature dedicated sections or stalls for rubber duck collectors. Check the event schedules and exhibitor lists to identify any showcasing rubber duck-related merchandise.

Local Toy Shops or Specialty Stores: Inquire at local toy shops or specialty stores that carry rubber ducks. Owners may be aware of regional events or know of collectors who organize meetups.

Rubber Duck Organizations: Keep an eye on organizations or groups that promote rubber duck awareness.

Annual Events and Festivals: Check the schedules of annual events or festivals in your region. Some festivals, especially those celebrating quirky or unique themes, may include rubber duck-related activities or conventions.

One notable event that has garnered attention for featuring a giant inflatable rubber duck is the "Giant Yellow Rubber Duck Project" by Dutch artist Florentijn Hofman. This ambitious project involves showcasing a massive inflatable rubber duck in various locations worldwide, attracting large crowds and extensive media coverage.

As we continue to explore the vibrant world of rubber duck collectors, stay tuned, where we'll delve even deeper into the quack-tastic stories, unique finds, and the everlasting charm that defines this extraordinary community. The rubber duck adventure sails on, promising more surprises and quack-filled wonders!

Conclusion

Our journey through the world of rubber ducks has been like a magical story unfolding. We started by discovering the history of these fun, floaty friends, imagining how they've changed over time and become a part of special moments.

Next, we splashed into the exciting world of rubber duck races, where these little quackers dash downstream, creating a river of joy. Each race is like a colorful adventure, from The Great Quack-Off Spectacle to The Grand Quackington Canal Race, bringing laughter and making a positive splash for good causes.

Now, as our rubber duck adventure wraps up, I invite you to have your own quack-tastic fun. Why not adopt a rubber duck, give it a name, and let it join you on your daily adventures? Create a little storybook of your duck's escapades, whether it's exploring your neighborhood, going on a road trip, or just enjoying bathtime fun.

So, keep quacking on, celebrate the simple joys, and let the whimsy of rubber ducks brighten your days. In a world that can sometimes be serious, these little ducks remind us to find joy in the quack-tastic moments that float into our lives. Happy quacking!

Draw a picture of a
rubber duck.

Draw a picture of a
rubber duck.

Printed in Great Britain
by Amazon

61753586R00020